ANIMALS
That Change the World!

Octopuses

Ashley Lee

Explore other books at:
WWW.ENGAGEBOOKS.COM

VANCOUVER, B.C.

e WWW.ENGAGEBOOKS.COM

Octopuses: Level 2
Animals That Change the World!
Lee, Ashley 1995 –
Text © 2020 Engage Books
Design © 2020 Engage Books

Edited by: A.R. Roumanis and Lauren Dick
Design by: A.R. Roumanis

Text set in Arial Regular.
Chapter headings set in Arial Black.

FIRST EDITION / FIRST PRINTING

LIBRARY AND ARCHIVES CANADA CATALOGUING IN PUBLICATION

Title: Octopuses: Animals That Change the World Level 2 reader / Ashley Lee
Names: Lee, Ashley, 1995- author

Identifiers: Canadiana (print) 20200309021 | Canadiana (ebook) 2020030903X
ISBN 978-1-77437-631-7 (hardcover)
ISBN 978-1-77437-759-8 (softcover)
ISBN 978-1-77437-633-1 (pdf)
ISBN 978-1-77437-634-8 (epub)
ISBN 978-1-77437-635-5 (kindle)

Subjects:
LCSH: Octopuses—Juvenile literature
LCSH: Human-animal relationships—Juvenile literature

Classification: QL430.3.O2 L44 2020 | DDC J594/.56—DC23

Contents

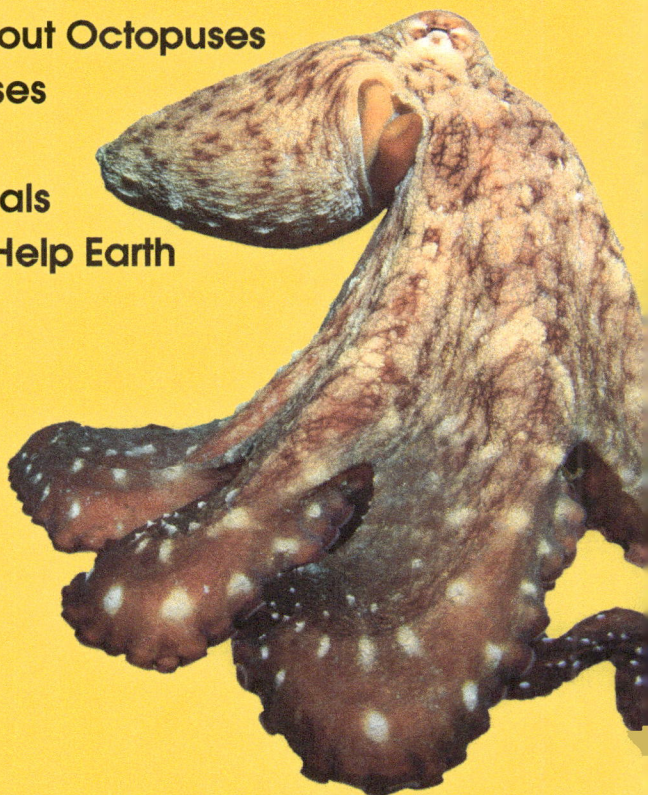

What Are Octopuses?

Octopuses are **cephalopods**. They are related to squid and cuttlefish. Octopuses have eight arms.

KEY WORD

Cephalopod: a smart and organized animal that lives in the ocean.

Octopuses mainly move by crawling on the bottom of the ocean. They are very helpful to people, other animals, and Earth.

A Closer Look

The smallest octopuses are wolfi octopuses. They are only 1 inch (2.5 centimeters) long. Giant Pacific octopuses are the largest octopuses. They can be up to 18 feet (5.4 meters) long.

Octopuses have suckers on their arms. Suckers help octopuses hold things.

Octopus eyes bulge out of their heads. The centers of their eyes are rectangle-shaped.

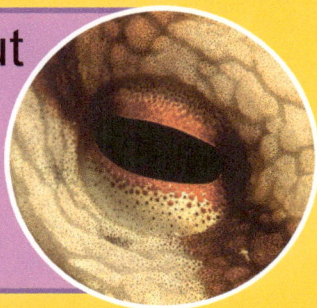

Octopuses have a hard beak. They use this to open shells.

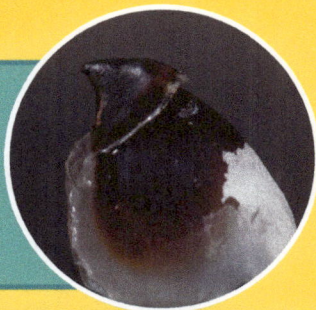

Where Do Octopuses Live?

Octopuses live in every ocean in the world. Most octopuses live alone. They make their homes in shells or in between rocks.

Caribbean reef octopuses are found near the Caribbean Sea. Capricorn night octopuses are mainly found off the Australian Coast. Curled octopuses live near the British Isles.

Arctic Ocean

British Isles

Europe

Australian coast

North America

Atlantic Ocean

Asia

Africa

Caribbean Sea

South America

Pacific Ocean

Australia

Southern Ocean

| 0 | 2,000 miles |
| 0 | 4,000 kilometers |

N

Legend
☐ Land
☐ Ocean

Antarctica

What Do Octopuses Eat?

Octopuses mainly eat crabs, shrimp, and **mollusks**. Octopuses use their suckers to smell their prey and trap them.

KEY WORD

Mollusks: animals with soft bodies and no bone in their backs. They are usually covered in a hard shell. Snails and clams are both mollusks.

Octopuses can use their beaks to inject **venom** into animals with shells. The venom makes it so the animal cannot move. The octopus can then open the shell easily.

How Do Octopuses Talk to Each Other?

Octopuses talk to each other by changing the color of their skin. An octopus showing dark colors likely wants to fight. Octopuses will also change color to hide from **predators**.

KEY WORD

Predators: animals that hunt other animals for food.

Octopuses use body language to talk to each other. They can stand up tall to make themselves look bigger to predators or reach towards another octopus.

Octopus Life Cycle

Octopuses can lay up to 100,000 eggs at one time. Female octopuses protect the eggs for several months until they are ready to **hatch**.

KEY WORD

Hatch: when a baby comes out of an egg.

Baby octopuses are called paralarvae. They are carried to the middle of the ocean by moving water called currents.

Octopuses grow into adults quickly by the time they reach the middle of the ocean. Most octopuses live for 3 to 5 years.

Curious Facts About Octopuses

Octopuses can regrow an arm if they lose one to a predator.

Octopuses release ink from their bodies when they are scared. This makes it hard for other animals to see.

Octopuses have three hearts.

Octopuses do not have bones. This helps them fit into small spaces.

Octopuses are skilled at escaping from tanks.

Octopuses have blue blood.

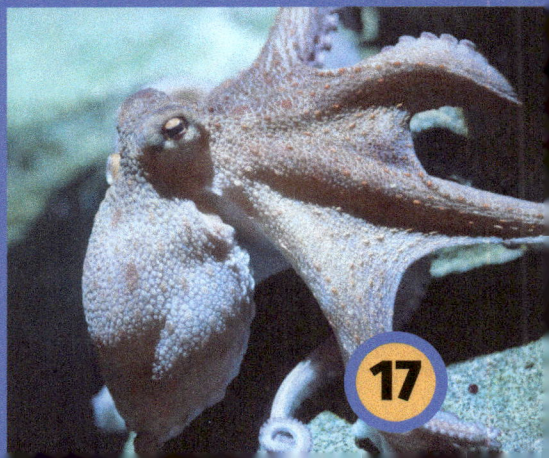

Kinds of Octopuses

There are about 300 different kinds of octopuses. Octopuses that live in deep water have fins. Octopuses that live in shallow water do not have fins.

Dumbo octopuses are only about 8 inches (20 cm) long. They have fins on their sides that look like ears.

Blue-ringed octopuses are one of the most dangerous animals in the ocean. Their venom is deadly.

Coconut octopuses gather coconut shells for shelter. They will carry coconut shells around the ocean.

How Octopuses Help Other Animals

Octopuses are an important food source for other animals. Birds, whales, and seals all eat octopuses.

These animals would not have as much food to eat without octopuses. They would start to disappear.

How Octopuses Help Earth

Octopuses are great recyclers. They use old items left by other animals to make new things.

Octopuses will make homes in old shells, wood, and even garbage. Some octopuses will put these items together to build bigger homes.

How Octopuses Help Humans

Scientists are working on creating new medicines from octopus venom.

They hope to make medicines to help with pain, allergies, and cancer.

Octopuses in Danger

Overfishing is when humans catch fish faster than new fish hatch. This leaves few fish left in the ocean. Overfishing means octopuses have less food to eat.

Lots of garbage ends up in oceans. Octopuses become sick if they try to eat garbage. Some octopuses may get hurt when they touch garbage.

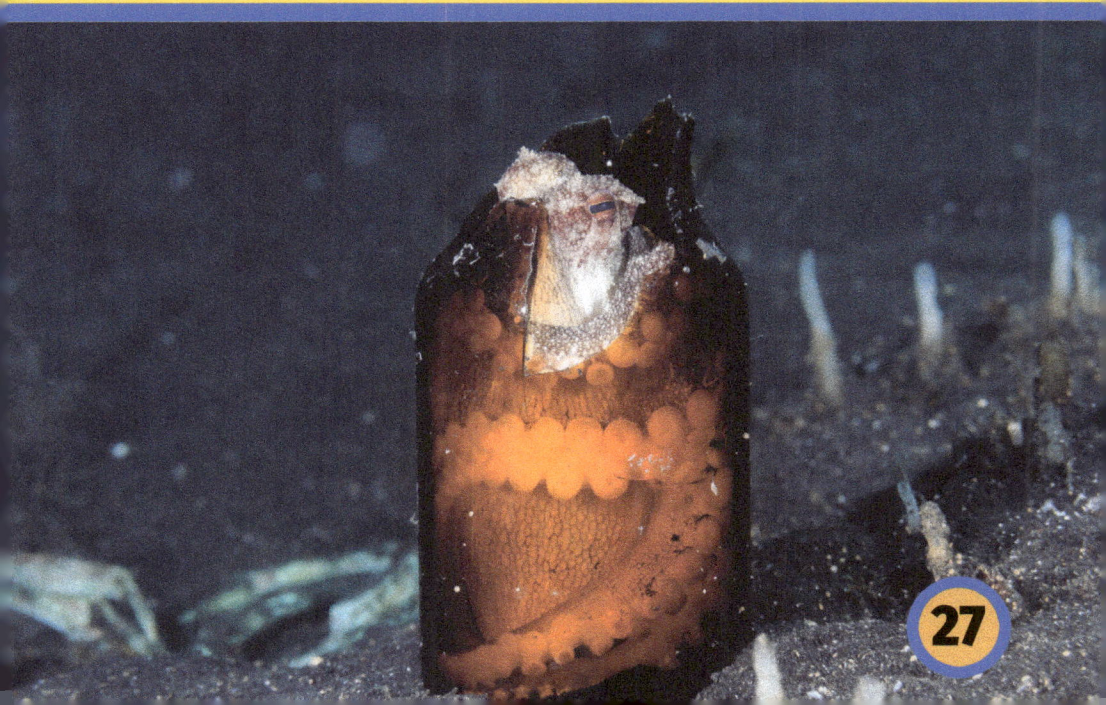

How To Help Octopuses

Household cleaners can end up in the ocean when they wash down the drain. These chemicals are harmful to octopuses. Many people are using soaps that are made from natural ingredients. Natural products will not harm sea life.

Lots of people organize ocean clean-ups with their friends and family. This keeps garbage out of oceans and protects octopuses.

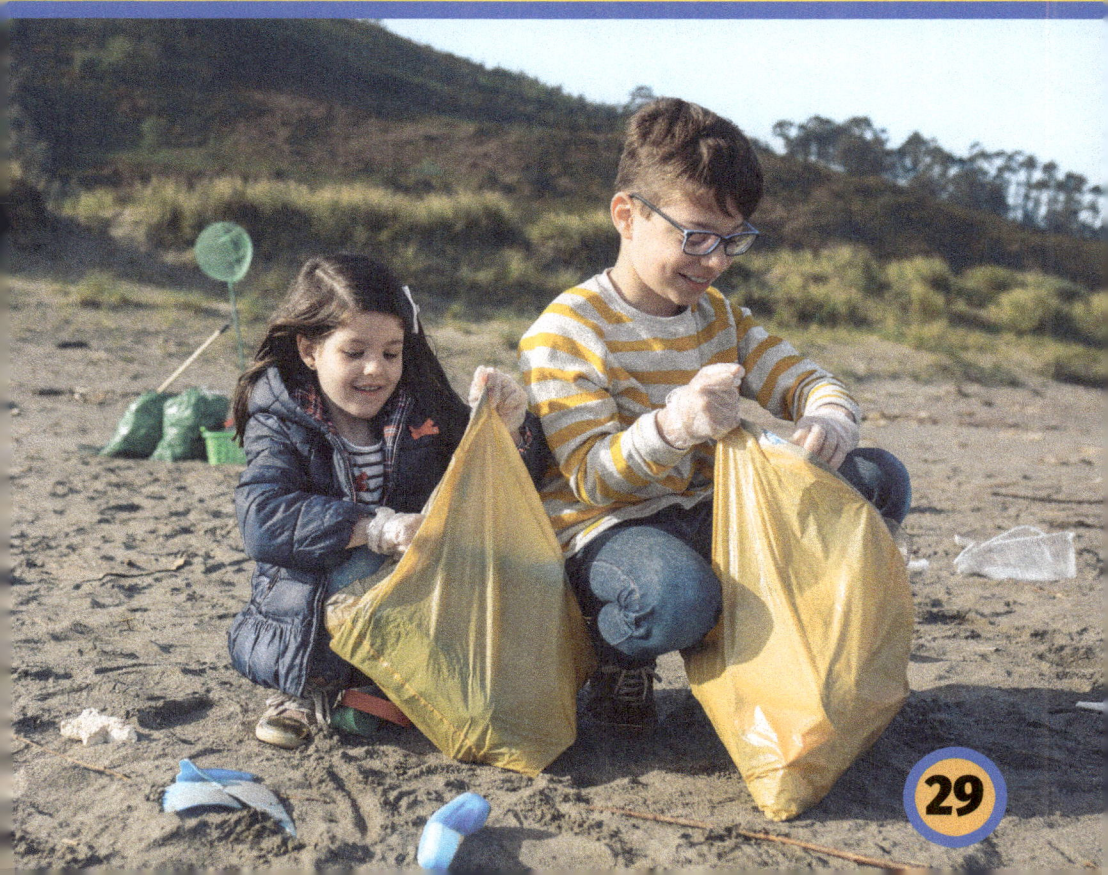

Quiz

Test your knowledge of octopuses by answering the following questions. The questions are based on what you have read in this book. The answers are listed on the bottom of the next page.

1 How many arms do octopuses have?

2 How do octopuses mainly move?

3 What are the smallest octopuses?

4 How long do octopuses live?

5 How many hearts do octopuses have?

6 What does overfishing mean for octopuses?

Explore other books in the Animals That Change the World series.

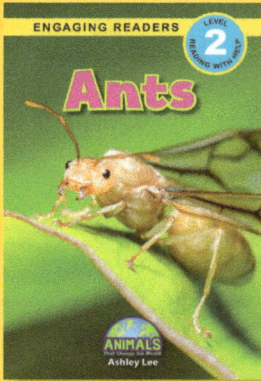

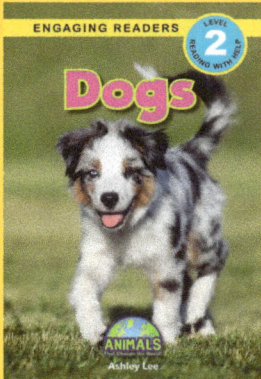

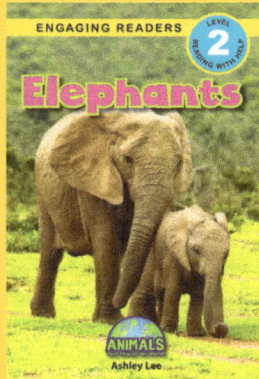

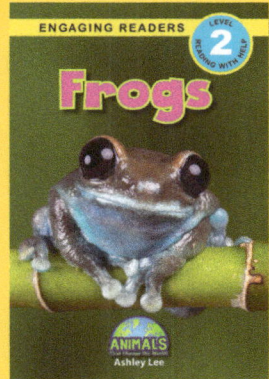

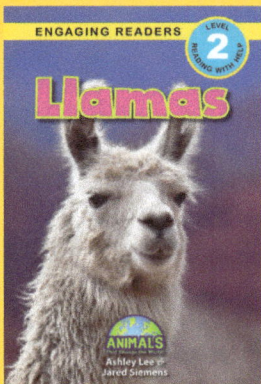

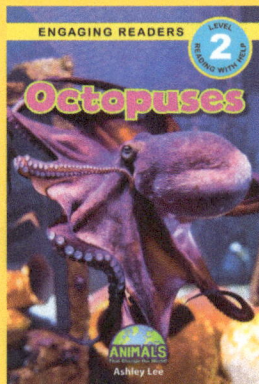

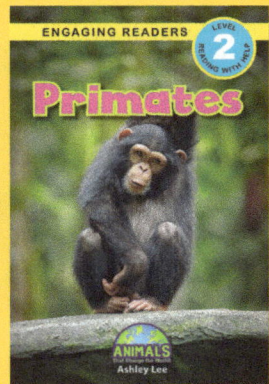

ENGAGING READERS — LEVEL 2 — READING WITH HELP
Ants
ANIMALS That Change the World
Ashley Lee

ENGAGING READERS — LEVEL 2 — READING WITH HELP
Beavers
ANIMALS That Change the World
Ashley Lee

ENGAGING READERS — LEVEL 2 — READING WITH HELP
Butterflies
ANIMALS That Change the World
Ashley Lee

ENGAGING READERS — LEVEL 2 — READING WITH HELP
Dogs
ANIMALS That Change the World
Ashley Lee

ENGAGING READERS — LEVEL 2 — READING WITH HELP
Elephants
ANIMALS That Change the World
Ashley Lee

ENGAGING READERS — LEVEL 2 — READING WITH HELP
Frogs
ANIMALS That Change the World
Ashley Lee

ENGAGING READERS — LEVEL 2 — READING WITH HELP
Llamas
ANIMALS That Change the World
Ashley Lee + Jared Siemens

ENGAGING READERS — LEVEL 2 — READING WITH HELP
Octopuses
ANIMALS That Change the World
Ashley Lee

ENGAGING READERS — LEVEL 2 — READING WITH HELP
Primates
ANIMALS That Change the World
Ashley Lee

Visit www.engagebooks.com to explore more Engaging Readers.

Answers: 1. Eight 2. By crawling on the bottom of the ocean 3. Wolf 4. 3 to 5 years 5. Three 6. They have less food to eat

31